Green Pigs & Me

By

Anna Mould

For my tribe; the incredible women who have
supported and encouraged me to make
this a reality.

My dear reader,

Thank you for choosing to read my story! It means so much to me that you will be sharing this journey and these pages with me.

This book is comprised of letters to my younger self, to a time when I was all-consumed by being everything to everyone, unable to discover an identity aside from those labels attached by others. In the years that have followed, there have been highs and lows – and that is life, as you know. There have been struggles relating to body image and self-worth; tempestuous moments in relationships, as well as times of joy, but all underpinned by the need to please others. As time has moved on, I have learned things about myself that I wish my younger self could know. Maybe it would give her hope or understanding as to why she made the choices she did.

My hope for you, dear reader, is that some of my journey will resonate, and that the words I offer to my younger self fall with you in a way that gives you hope as well.

With much love,

Anna x x

"We don't often get to choose what scars we get, but we do get to choose how we see them and what we do with them."

(S. C. Lourie)

My darling Anna,

You are probably wondering what I'm doing writing letters to you, my younger self. I see you now, just turned thirty. You couldn't celebrate your birthday as your youngest son, eight months old, was in hospital with cellulitis. You started your new job about six weeks beforehand and are wondering what your new boss must be thinking!

Your twenties were a rollercoaster of different relationships, getting to grips with your career as a nurse, with motherhood, homemaking and trying to be everything to everyone.

What about you?

The next fifteen years are not easy. Work is challenging, motherhood even more so. And that question – what about you? – remains at the back of your mind for a long time. I am writing to tell you things I wish I had known – wish you had known at the time now that I have lived through it. I have had time to reflect and want to send you words of support, encouragement, love and hope.

Life continues to be a challenge, my love, but in a much more fulfilling and inspiring way. You may feel lost now, but you begin to discover yourself, I promise. And in doing so, you begin to find peace.

The first thing I learned the hard way and wish for you to know now: you cannot pour from an empty cup.

You cannot continue to be everything to everyone, and you will learn to take care of you. You remember that you are important too. You are the most important person to love and nourish. You just need to give yourself permission to do so.

With so much love
X x

It's Okay to Stop

My darling Anna,

Well, this is a rare occurrence! I'm out of bed at 6a.m. which, as you know, is not something I would keenly volunteer to do. Sleep is something you crave at thirty, although the baby's nights will get easier as he grows. One thing you and I are good at, and relish, is napping. And you will come to a place where you no longer feel guilty for resting.

As I write, we are in the midst of a pandemic (there's a sentence I never thought I'd write!). Coronavirus put the world in lockdown, and although the UK is gingerly taking steps to reopen businesses, things are far from normal. What the lockdown has enforced, and I have found a blessing in disguise, is a slower pace of living.

Why rush? There is nothing to rush for.

A silver lining of the crisis has been having to stay home (which for an introvert is not a huge ask), and I have enjoyed more opportunities to "be" rather than "do" all the time. I have been able to write to you, for example. I have done some painting, something I never thought I was any good at. I have read some great books by incredible women – something I know you wish you had the time to do.

Please don't think this change of pace happened easily overnight. I can hear you shouting at me "How have you got the time to paint? I barely have time to pee!" And I remember what that was like. It has taken me a couple of years to recognise that I need to – and give myself permission to – slow down and stop trying to please everyone. This is a big thing for you and me. Two years of counselling at the right time helps me to finally see that we can never be all things to all people, and that trying to be is making me ill.

A few years ago, we were trying to do it all. Full-time job. Mother. Daughter. Wife. Sister. Friend. Step-mum. Trying to make sure everyone was happy and trying to be happy ourselves. On the outside, we were! Off on adventures, grasping every opportunity that came our way to be out and about, trying new things. We did have a lot of fun, we really did.

I was discussing this time with the older boy this week (can you believe he's nearly twenty?!). He said that he knew I was doing all these things to be happy, but he was so unhappy at times. He missed me, needed me to be home. The guilt and shame that I felt at the time and when talking to him – I must have been a terrible mum, not being there when he needed me. I was a bad person, not a good enough parent. He struggled a great deal with secondary school, and it is only when he gets to college that we discover he is dyslexic and has ADHD. We could have done with having that information five years earlier; relationships would have been so much easier, and it would have saved a great deal of heartache.

Here lies the crux of the matter. Home was hard. Emotionally painful at times, again trying to keep everyone happy, playing referee and diplomat. Doing exciting things like dancing, having days out or weekends away was an escape. A distraction. Another persona to step into.

You always had to come home.

I was working full-time, out several nights a week. I was anxious about upsetting others, walking on eggshells much of the time. I was exhausted. I wasn't really giving my best to anyone – friends, family, colleagues, least of all to myself.

So, I stopped.

I upset someone hugely, something I wish I could have handled differently, as I caused a great deal of hurt, but at the time I didn't know how. I went into self-protection mode, almost the 'fear paralysis' response (when you are faced with a perceived danger, your body will go into either fight, flight or freeze mode. Freezing conserves physical energy even though the adrenaline is still pumping. This freezing can still lead to high anxiety, as that energy is still within you).

Since stopping, I have rested a great deal. As I said, I went through two years of counselling, and almost needed permission to not do for everyone all the time. And it's ok. Everyone is still breathing. I am still breathing.

Breathing deeply.

I want you to know that you can stop. You can have that time out. I know you fear asking for time for yourself, but it is ok. You can rest when baby's sleeping. You can go to bed at 8p.m. instead of catching up with housework. You need to take care of you because living on anxiety is exhausting.

By not taking that time just for you, you will lose sight of what is important for you. Opportunities may come and go, but what I have learned during this pandemic is that joy can be found in the everyday. You don't have to fear missing out on life, as life is what you make it. You don't have to go far to find something that touches your soul.

You just have to stop and listen for it.

With love,
X x

In Search of Happiness

My dear Anna,

Today I am writing to you from my favourite corner of my local park. It's next to the old Victorian public library building, overlooking the flower beds. I can hear the bees humming around the lavender. It's very peaceful, as we're still under the social distancing rules of Covid 19 lockdown, and most people are over by the playpark. Today, I am feeling truly happy! I don't know what has shifted, but I have an overwhelming feeling of joy and lightness, and I can't stop smiling!

My younger self, you do experience happiness – this is not a totally alien emotion or state, but happiness often depended on others. We made others responsible for 'making us' happy, and I think that's why early relationships failed.

Getting married at nineteen was supposed to 'make you' happy, but you soon realised that was not the case. You quickly grew apart as you developed and discovered more about yourself – particularly whilst completing your training as a mental health nurse. You soon realised that you didn't even really like the man you were with, let alone want to spend the rest of your life with him. (Sidenote, if you had stayed with him, this would have been your Silver Anniversary year. Scary thought). In short, he didn't 'make you happy'.

Your next partner, who you adored, was a very different person. You had a lot of fun... a lot of alcohol... and a lot of sex! Eighteen months in, with six months of living together, he no longer 'made you' happy, and you were distracted by someone else who was kind, made you laugh, 'made you' feel special and loved. This time, you were the one on the pedestal, which was not a nice place to be. You were responsible for someone else's happiness, security and mental wellbeing. You couldn't deliver. You had a child with this man, who was such a blessing, but this gave you another layer of responsibility. You were mothering two, depended upon for financial and emotional stability when the world around you appeared to be falling apart and no one else could see it. You felt like you were screaming into a chasm, but no one could hear you. You loved this man, but you couldn't save both of you. You met someone. He 'made you' feel special and loved. Maybe he could 'make you' happy? You picked up your child and bolted for safety.

At thirty, you are married again, with a second child. You are a step-mum to three. You are working full-time in your new job. Waiting for something to 'make you' happy.

Please don't misunderstand, you do have happiness in your life. My message is that no one else will 'make you' happy. Not partners, not children, not friends. You can and will experience happiness with them, or course you will. For a long time however, everything else seems to take priority. Including their happiness.

Find what gives you joy. What makes your heart sing? YOUR heart.

Something I am now aware that I have done over the years is to embrace what makes those I love happy. Boundaries have never been easy. Morphing into what you think the other person wants means that when you start becoming yourself, the other person doesn't know what's happening. Keeping to the mould you make for yourself for each person causes anxiety; it is exhausting and leads to resentment because you are suppressing your true being, and you feel you are not good enough. Some of what made others happy has aligned with what you enjoy, and experiencing new things is fun, but putting aside something calling your heart to make time to keep others happy is stifling. I was never aware I was doing it at the time, but with the benefit of hindsight, it is clear. It is linked to our need to be liked and accepted, and by pleasing those around us, those whose happiness is important to us, we made ourself less of a priority.

Listen to your heart. What does it say? At forty-four, I can say I am a painter, a writer, a singer, a dancer, a yogi, a gardener, a nature lover. I am passionate in my career; I am a specialist in my field. I am a mother, wife, daughter, sister, nana, friend, colleague, mentor, teacher. And I am happy. Believe you will be happy.

With love
X x

From Novice to Specialist

Dear Anna,

I wanted to pause and talk to you as I have just presented my first online teaching session for the Facebook group I co-admin for non-medical prescribers in mental health (you won't be on Facebook for another couple of years, you couldn't see what the fuss was all about! You are now leading an international group in your speciality). My reason for wanting to talk to you now is to show you how far you have come.

I remember the first day as a qualified nurse – what had we done! As a green, young nurse fresh from university, you work on a new ward with a team recently moved from the old county asylum – where routines and rituals had not changed for decades. You were never going to win big. However, it was a place to start to develop your skills and you fall in love with dementia care.

You moved around, changed jobs – a short spell in a nursing home (more routines and rituals), a day hospital, which you enjoyed, and now at thirty, you're about to embark on the role that pretty much makes the nurse I am today. You have joined an established team, and the Memory Clinic becomes your forte. You develop your craft, build on your skills, and undertake a University course to become a prescriber. You qualify through dedication and hard work (your boys are only seven and three!). As the service shifts and changes, you undertake a leadership role (I know, I was as surprised as you!), and ultimately you spend three years as the team leader. The team become family, and some colleagues are cherished friends even now. Sadly, the job becomes larger but the number of hours in the day stay the same. I remember feeling I had failed or was letting the team down, when in fact the culture of wanting 'more for less' meant the management were taking and taking from me. The expectations became huge. You become exhausted, and there seems to be little time for life away from work. You surprise yourself in 2015 by applying for a completely different job. A band lower on the pay scale, but a new challenge. It breaks your heart to say goodbye to the team you have worked with for nearly ten years but if you don't say goodbye, you will be broken.

The new role presented many challenges, a vertical learning curve working in an acute hospital working in older adults' mental health.

You thrive.

You continue to prescribe, and you carve your own path. You present at conferences, both locally and nationally. You have a paper published. This year, you have been promoted to Clinical Specialist, and you soon will be embarking on an Advanced Practice programme.

This in itself comes with some pressures and expectations – mostly perceived rather than real. I am the guinea pig for the team, the first to embark on this career path. My supervisor is a consultant psychiatrist for whom I have so much respect and admiration. What if I fail? What if I look like an idiot? What if it is beyond my scope of knowledge, and I can't meet the expectations of the programme?

But… what if I fly? I will have the opportunity to carve a new role and career path. The prospect of the course is both exciting and terrifying. I have the support of my colleagues, my husband, my family and friends. I have to believe in me.

I wonder if that naïve nineteen-year-old, embarking on her nursing career straight from sixth form college, ever envisaged how the journey would pan out; whether she truly believed that she could do it?

I am so proud of you for keeping going, for daring to make changes, taking on new skills, saying 'yes' to scary things. You will love where your job takes you – the people you meet, the lives you touch and those that touch yours. Nursing is truly a privilege, seeing people at their most vulnerable and being able to make even the smallest positive change. We are blessed to do what we do.

Keep going, my girl,
X x

"If you're always trying to be normal, you will never know how amazing you can be."

(Maya Angelou)

Bucking the Body Image Trend pt1

Darling Anna,

I am writing to you today from a cool oasis. The Turkish restaurant has opened their courtyard garden. Beautiful surroundings, with grapes on the vine overhead, flowering hanging baskets. The sky is blue, and I am sitting in a shaded area in the corner, enjoying a cool breeze and a delicious coffee.

I wanted to write to you today about your – my – body. I know, at thirty, you are thrilled to have lost weight after your second baby. You are the lowest weight you have been since being in the grips of bulimia ten years previously. You are the smallest dress size you have ever been. Yet, you still feel inadequate. Sub-standard. Fat. Unattractive. Unworthy.

You learned from a young age that fat=bad; less-than; ugly; wrong. I had a conversation with Mum this morning about some old photos she had found of herself growing up, from baby years to grammar school. "I started off quite cute but ended up fat and 'orrible". Mum is tall and does have a larger frame, but "'orrible"? Never. You grew up watching her write down every morsel that passed her lips. A5 folders filled with hundreds of daily calorific records. 'X' food is good, 'Y' food is bad. Numbers on the page could not exceed the golden target, or that was 'naughty'. Much-loved foods were 'treats' on a good day. It was natural that, at fourteen or fifteen, you started monitoring the number of calories that passed your lips.

At junior school, you were picked on because of your 'fat' mum. You were called 'fat' by the popular girls. They were pretty, they went to dance classes. You envied their sateen leotards and tights that they wore for some PE classes. Mum relented and took you to the dancewear specialist shop. Black leotard, red tights. You loved them. Until you wore them for PE.

"Hippo!" Not only were you fat, but they were the wrong ones. Mocked, yet again, by the popular girls.

You quickly gained weight at college (hello, alcohol!), and felt like the token 'fat girl' on nights out. But that was ok, right? You had a boyfriend and weren't out to meet men. You lost weight for your wedding at nineteen. At twenty-one, when you were coming to the end of your nurse training and hugely anxious about starting your first job. You realised you were miserable in your marriage and wanted out. You developed bulimia and binge-eating as a way of having some degree of control over what was happening in your life. Your weight plummeted. You were highly anxious, but people commented on how 'well' and 'good' you looked. You were suddenly acceptable to society. The popular girls wouldn't have called you a hippo now!

You meet someone new. He loves your body. You begin your recovery from the behaviours of bulimia and binging. Hardly unsurprisingly, you begin to gain a little weight. I vividly remember being naked in the kitchen with him, making breakfast together (naked cooking… oh to be young again). He stood behind you and wrapped him arms around your waist, traced his hand across your lower belly and commented "oh, this is growing a bit".

Devastated.

Gaining weight = drawing attention = losing sex appeal for your partner = unlovable = need to diet.

And so begins the story of your twenties. Calorie counting, constant self-judgement and criticism. "You shouldn't be eating that, you pig." Salads in restaurants, anxious about what fellow diners thought. Desperately needing validation from your partner. Needing needing needing.

You meet someone who makes you feel beautiful and wants you as you are.

You fell pregnant fairly quickly and – oh, shocker! – your body changed. As soon as you gave birth, you were thinking about losing weight. I remember having a shower in the maternity unit, and in the wet room, directly opposite the shower cubicle, was a full-length mirror. There you stood, two days post-partum, boobs leaking, bleeding, staring at your ravaged body, crying.

You had a beautiful baby, and all you could think about were your stretchmarks and excess fat. You counted points daily, writing everything down. Judging your worth based on the decreasing number on the scale. Dieting continued.

Celebrity magazines – what a great idea they were! "You should look like this!" "Ooo dear, she's still fat six months after giving birth!" "OH MY GOD! She's got cellulite!" "How awful does she look in this dress?!" Judging others and comparing yourself to the impossible ideal became an obsession. You were aware of the impact this may also have on your step-daughters – the last thing you wanted was for them to grow obsessed with their bodies as you had been, self-critical to the point of purging or trying to make themselves smaller, concentrate all their time and energy on what they looked like rather than grow into their fullest potential. You didn't want them to pick up on or imitate your habits. You felt your worth depended on your approval under the male gaze (another trait you didn't want them to develop). And when your male had been unable to give you that approval or validation, you sought it elsewhere.

Now you are thirty, with baby number two. Still obsessed, still critical of yourself. Still censoring your appetite. Things will change, my love. They will. You go through a period of transformation. Supported by incredible women, you learn to see your worth as separate from your body shape and size. You learn to see that you matter, and that your happiness is as important as that of your loved ones. You try new things which give you freedom from the restrictions of "I'm too big to…" and "I'm not good enough to…". Dancing, burlesque, photoshoots. You step onto the stage with your alter ego and you feel amazing. Without having to lose 10lb before you try.

At forty-four, I am more content in my skin than ever. I am probably the largest I have been in terms of dress size. I have no idea what I weigh. I wear clothes that bring me joy and are comfortable to wear – largely unconventional by high street standards, but life's too short to wear boring clothes, right? I feel free to do it because I no longer give a shit about the male gaze or conforming to society's standard of beauty. I no longer care what others think. I am happy. At forty-four, I have posed naked in a forest for an incredibly empowering photoshoot. It was magical and liberating. I felt at home. And happy.

Don't misunderstand me, those foodie demons are not dead. They are alive and kicking, and still like to have their say. Now, I talk back. I question their logic. I thank them for their concern and reassure them that it's all fine. And it works, most of the time. I had a big wobble a couple of years ago, when I did the Snowdonia zipwire with Hubby. They need to know your weight for safety when strapping you to the wire. Fair enough. They weigh you one at a time – in front of everyone – and write the number of kilograms on your wristband in thick black ink. As I said, I don't know what I weigh – haven't for years – but it was a big number. It felt like a badge of shame. Everyone could see. I resisted the urge to mentally convert kilos to stones, but I knew it was a big number.

At the time, I felt even more anxious about that number than I did about being thrown from a mountain in a body bag! The number sat with me for some time. I resisted going back to my old ways.

I no longer care.

I may be bigger now, but I can still do my job. I can do yoga, I can dance. I can walk along the beach. I can climb a hill. I can run around with my grandbabies. My family don't love me any less – have they even noticed? I am happy in my own skin. You will be happy in your own skin. Don't waste your hours and your brilliant mind with working out the calories in that cake. Eat the cake. Enjoy it. The company you share your enjoyment of the cake with, they love you. For you. They enjoy your company. They don't care about your dress size. And if they do? Well. You'll be happier without a friendship that's dependent on aesthetics. You are more than a number on a scale. You really are.

Sending so much love,
X x

Bucking the Body Image Trend pt2

My dear girl,

My relationship with my body has been a love/hate one over the years, and this has largely been fuelled by external voices and influences. If the male gaze approved, my body must have been "good". If I lost weight, "good". If I fit in a smaller clothing size, "good". Food restriction, "good". Feeling hungry, "good". I even delayed stopping smoking as I was worried about gaining weight. If my body is the home of my soul, why have I punished it? Why have I berated myself, over and over, in ways I would never talk to someone I love?

You have two children – how amazing is that? Your body kept two humans alive, protecting, growing, and nourishing them. I remember our youngest, at about four or five, climbing on the sofa next to you for a cuddle. He rubbed your belly and said, "You've had a lot to eat today!"

Out of the mouths of babes. I was fat.

He then went on to say, "I like your tummy, it's soft and nice to cuddle." My heart melted.

Your body has worked as it should since you were born. You are so lucky. It has been abused, starved, been made to purge itself. And it kept going.

I am grateful that, in my forties, my body still works. Aches and pains are usually remedied through gentle exercise, rest, massage, or sessions with the osteopath (you will learn the joys of seeing the bone cruncher – its heavenly torture!). Recently, I have had investigations for bowel issues, which could be Irritable Bowel Syndrome. Never be embarrassed about your body and its normal functions – by seeing my G.P. and having investigations, a polyp was biopsied. Thankfully, it was benign but had the potential to become cancerous. Further investigations are to make sure there are no others lurking. If I had been embarrassed about poo, I could have developed bowel cancer. Simple as that. IBS isn't exactly a Mardi Gras, but its manageable and non-life threatening.

When I look in the mirror these days, I don't pick holes in my appearance. I don't love everything about my body. Some days I think I'm smaller that I actually am. My belly is rounded. I have many stretchmarks. My upper arms are quite big. I have more than one chin. I also have beautiful long hair. My blue eyes change colour with my mood. I like my smile and my dimples. I try to say nice things to myself about how I look. I don't hate my body anymore. I accept it now for how it looks and thank it for what it can do.

My body is merely the home for my soul. It needs to be cared for if I am to fulfil my dreams. By not obsessing negatively over my body, I can focus on positively moving forward and nurture my life.

X x

"What is the greatest lesson a woman should learn? That since day one she's already had everything she needs within herself. It's the world that convinced her she did not."

(Rupi Kaur)

Friendship and Fitting In

Dear Anna,

Friendship's a funny ol' thing, isn't it? There is the saying, "Friendships last for a reason, a season or a lifetime." You rarely know which it will be when you embark on the journey, and some will surprise you.

Do you remember junior school? There were girls who were your friends. Girls who said they were your friends but treated you badly. The popular girls who you wished were your friends despite them treating you badly. You were desperate for their approval, to the point you would make things up so they would like you, but they knew you were lying so would treat you like shit even more. Senior school wasn't much better, although you met a broader group of people. But your clothes were wrong on non-uniform day. And you weren't very sporty. Or 'pretty'. Or popular.

College, well, a bit of an alcohol-fuelled mess, really. A new group of friends, largely male. You met your husband-to-be just after starting college, so no student romances for you. Again, a few real friends, plenty of drinking associates. You felt happier going out with one group of friends – the males, because there was no pressure to conform or perform. Your female friends would go out elsewhere, mainly to find a bed mate. You hated those meat-market nightclubs. You felt like the "fat friend" because the girls you went with seemed more confident and sexually appealing. They fitted in. You never felt like you fitted in.

University was next, and you made one good friend, as well as largely getting on with the group. You were the baby on the nursing course, especially the mental health cohort. There were cliques – you were young but didn't live in halls so didn't fit in that group. You got married, so didn't often socialise with young single colleagues. In the final couple of months of training, you develop an intense friendship with a girl also struggling with an eating disorder (by this time, you were bulimic). You support each other, but one day she ups and moves away without warning, not finishing the course. You feel abandoned.

You make more friends on your first ward when you qualify, but you were a trained nurse – friendships with junior staff were frowned upon as that could lead to problems on the shop floor if you were taking charge. You were the youngest trained nurse, newly separated from your husband, joining an established team. You didn't quite fit in.

Over the next twelve or so years, your friends were largely work colleagues or friends of your partner/husband. Outside of work you are a mum, essentially. You didn't fit in with the school gate mums, as you weren't born and bred in this town. When you find friendship, you go all in.

It's an intense relationship, someone you are in awe of. She highlights to you how you need to consider your own needs – she's right! – and she shows the way. You have amazing opportunities and new experiences - dancing, burlesque, theatre. You develop a deep bond, and you begin making this your priority. Along the way, you meet other incredible women and experience wonderful things. Some of these connections get lost with time as relationships fall apart. Some of these women hurt your friend, and you stay loyal to her, support her. That's what good friends do, right? You have to reassure her that you are not going to be someone who lets her down or makes her feel abandoned or rejected. Ultimately, though, this is what happens. You give your time, money, attention and energy to supporting the dreams of your friend. She is the first person you text every day. Every. Day. You find yourself feeling guilty if you don't. She's your best friend, why wouldn't you be in constant contact? You find yourself taking days off work to support her with her projects, which you gladly do. Weekends off are taken up with exciting adventures.

She often comments about your marriage and family life, and how Hubby and the boys don't really like her. All kids love her! She comments how you haven't involved her in your family or your life. You make suggestions of things to do with them, which are rebuffed. Can't she see that you're managing your life to prioritise her?

You attend all her classes, to support her and her ventures, and feel guilty if you can't go because, for example, you need to be with your children. You make yourself go even when you're exhausted, as you don't want to let her down.

You begin listening to her comments about your relationships with others – Hubby, your children, your stepchildren, your family, other friends. They eat away at you, making you uncertain of your connections. And you believe that her friendship is the only relationship that matters. It is the centre of your world.

You start "doing things wrong", and she openly tells you. You receive messages detailing how you've upset her. You know you are far from perfect and would never intentionally hurt her. Some comments are fair, and you can see how your actions may have been taken that way. You find yourself analysing your messages to her, and mentally dissecting conversations to pinpoint the key errors. When sending messages, you re-write them several times, anxious to be saying things in a way that cannot be misconstrued. You hit send, and then wait expectantly and nervously for a reply, as this will set the tone for the rest of your day.

All the while, you are still trying to manage a career, a marriage, motherhood, and family life. You try to balance a million spinning plates whilst walking on eggshells, but you cannot keep it going. You begin having irrational thoughts about others, fuelled by planted expectations –

how others perceive you should be treated or how you should manage things. Granted, some of the situations do need to be rectified, but you need to work it out for yourself, in your own time. You don't want to let anyone down. Grandchildren arrive – another plate. More expectations planted.

And then it comes. You are not supporting your friend in the way they need or expect. You should know she needs more from you, should know what to give. You get it wrong. Again.

SMACK.

My heart is in my mouth. Shaking.

How could I have got it wrong? She really needed my support and understanding. I had been trying to keep everyone happy, doing what I thought they wanted/needed. I was missing the mark for everyone, it seemed. I wasn't giving my friend the support she needed. I wasn't present enough in my family. I wasn't present for me. Feelings of guilt and shame poured in again. I had let everyone down. I wasn't a good enough friend, mother, wife.

So, I loosened my grip on what I had been prioritising – the friendship, terrified of what would happen if I let go completely. She would hate me. I had proved myself to be an awful friend, just like everyone else who had let her down.

But as I loosened my grip, I felt anxiety loosen its grip around my throat.

I could breathe.

I could stop.

Friendships since then have not been easy. I have realised that the women I grew friendly with in that circle were not my true friends. They were her friends. I am struggling to trust friendships developing too deeply. I resist going "all in" as I don't want to hurt anyone again. I know I hurt my friend very much and I regret that that was the outcome. I didn't know what else to do at the time.

I have learned the hard way that many relationships, both romantic and platonic, have ended not because I no longer loved the person but because, as a people-pleaser, I didn't put in place or reinforce boundaries. I wanted to be everything to another person, to care for and support them, "make them" happy, to the point of exhaustion and being no longer able to meet the expectations of the relationship. Should relationships have such expectations? I was unable to keep up my "end of the bargain", as the other person saw it. I was trying to keep so many other bargains at the same time. When I have connected with individuals who are important to me, I have put them on a pedestal and wanted to be my best for them. I need to be the best for myself, first.

I have made connections with other women since without expectation, without trying to anticipate where the relationship will lead. And so far, so good! It feels like a safe circle where we can all voice our worries and successes, and they are met with love and support, without judgement. I have re-connected with some friends I had lost. I am making friends with myself, being present for me and discovering my needs and desires. And they are quite different to what I thought!

I also have cherished friends who I can go weeks or months without seeing, and the relationship doesn't suffer. We pick up where we left off, we still talk about important things, confide in each other, and know that the other is there for us should we need them. Just because we don't speak daily or weekly our friendship is not diminished, nor does it make that connection less important in my life.

Make friends, please, but remain grounded in what you need, remain connected to your dreams and desires. Learn to create the boundaries that I was unable to. They get lost so easily in trying to keep others happy.

X x

"Every new beginning comes from some other beginning's end."

(Semisonic)

Loss & Letting Go

Darling Anna,

The ending of any relationship, whether platonic or romantic, is a loss. Following the recent loss of a good friend, who you loved deeply, you went through a period of mourning. It's strange that the breakdown of romantic relationships is openly talked about, written about, they have albums of songs dedicated to their ending, but not so for friendships.

I have said before about how your letting go of this friendship allowed you to breathe again and that your anxiety lessened, but this was replaced by a deep sadness. You had lost that bond; the relationship had shifted so greatly that it could never be the same. You didn't have the emotional energy or skills to rebuild, so you let it slip away. You "readily gave up", as your friend told you. It was a bereavement, a grieving process. You went through stages of anger, largely toward yourself for "getting it so wrong". There was sadness as you remembered all the amazing chapters of your friendship, how it grew and where it took you. You grieved the loss of potential future chapters. You were bitter toward yourself. Why couldn't you have done more? Tried harder? Given more? Been more?

I am now left with a feeling of gratitude to the friendship that was, to the time we had together and what I have learned along the way about myself. The anger is gone now, but I am still working through the uncertainty about new friendships, not going in too deep too soon. Can I trust them with my fears and secrets? Some old anxieties easily creep up – "why hasn't she texted me back? Have I upset her? What have I done or said that could have been wrong?". Dissecting everything that I have done or said is not a healthy ingredient to any relationship, as I found the hard way. I have to give myself a good talking to some days – "it's not about me". There have been other lost friendships along the way, either through choice or circumstance. Looking back, few were a considered decision to end a friendship, but cutting one cord often leads to others being severed too.

I think during our twenties, we did not allow ourselves the time to grieve the loss of former relationships. One man to the next to the next. No room for sadness – we couldn't have our new man thinking we missed the last one! As I have written before, you often still had love for them, but didn't feel they were "making you" happy. You didn't leave because you stopped loving them, you left because you needed more. You didn't know how to be what you needed for yourself. Low self-esteem and self-worth hinged on how others related to you. It takes a lot of work, my love, but you will find a place where you no longer wait for the approval or permission of others to be you. Glorious, messy, beautiful you. However you choose to be.

Take time to mourn the loss of past loves, of friendships ended too soon. Celebrate the joy shared, the lessons learned. This will help you move forward in new relationships and in helping others do the same.

X x

"Everything you've ever wanted is on
the other side of fear."

(George Addair)

The Roots of Fear & Staying Small

My darling Anna,

This is going to be hard to write, and equally hard for you to read, I would imagine. These events have been buried away in that part of the memory that says "painful: do not open". I'm writing to you about them as I believe these events shaped and influenced the majority of our future relationships with men, definitely, and other general behaviours – feeling unable to breathe in crowded spaces; needing to be able to easily escape from situations; always having to have my back to a wall in a lift or on a busy train. Avoidance of conflict in all relationships, wanting to please everyone. Fear at the thought of speaking your truth, even to those you love and who love you. Fear of upsetting anyone. One of these events I only recalled in recent years, and it blindsided me. Talking it over with my counsellor helped me to begin to heal.

When you were sixteen, do you remember that older guy who you met at your Saturday job? He and his friends were customers. You probably wouldn't have made a date if your work colleagues hadn't encouraged you. They didn't know he was twelve years older than you, a habitual cannabis user and drinker, or that he was controlling and paranoid. They wanted you to have a date! You were young and naïve, and wanted to keep him happy as part of you was scared. One night, at the shared house he lived in, he raped you. He held a barber's straight-edged razor to your neck with the threat of drawing blood if you made a sound.

You didn't make a sound. You didn't move. Frozen. Eyes closed, waiting for him to get bored.

On other occasions, he would force-feed you alcohol. One night, the night before a family holiday, your parents were so worried when you didn't come home that they sent the police to the house. You were more scared of what he would do if you answered the door, so you hid. The police stopped knocking. You went to bed with him and because you were on your period and he wouldn't take no for an answer, when you woke it was like a blood bath. You quickly washed and left before he woke up. He thought it was funny – when you dutifully phoned him, he said he thought he had killed you. Hilarious. On another night, he didn't give you a chance to remove your tampon. You needed to go to A&E to have it retrieved and removed.

Thankfully, he moved back to his hometown. He was angry when you said you wouldn't be following him there, as you were about to start college. Apparently, he was going to ask you to "come off the pill". Can you imagine?!

He was only the second man you had slept with. The first had been just a year or two older than you, and he had only wanted a virgin. You had been infatuated with that one. And so, the journey into adulthood began, believing men only wanted sex, that that was the way to gain their approval and attention, and that this is all you would be able to offer. Within two weeks of starting college and socialising (pubs!) with a wider circle, you met the man you would marry at nineteen. He was eight years your senior, in the Navy when you met him, and after just fourteen days together, he went away for six months to the Gulf. Whilst he was away, there was the odd drunken kiss, and a one-night stand with an ex-boyfriend from school. It was during these six months that you began going to nightclubs with some of your college friends, and it was on one of these nights that you were assaulted.

It was a promotion night for Ann Summers, I think, and you were stood with a couple of male friends from college, just dancing and watching the show. One of these friends was initially stood behind you with his hands on your hips. You became aware that he was then stood next to you, but someone else's hands were on your hips.

Then one was on your arse.

At the hem of your skirt.

Pulling down your tights, inside your underwear.

Inside you.

You freeze to the spot.

His other hand pulls you to him, his erection is against you through both your clothes.

His fingers are still inside you.

Pain.

You can smell his breath.

Beer and cigarettes, acrid and warm.

Everyone around you is oblivious. Dancing, drinking, smiling.

Suddenly, the show is over, and you are free from his grasp. You turn and are faced with his chest. Don't look up.

You push past, pushing through so many bodies until you reach the toilets. In the cubicle, you assess the situation. You're bleeding.

He made you bleed.

You are cheap. Dirty. Just a body, a plaything. Disposable.

When I talked this through with my counsellor, she asked, "What did you do next?"

I got cleaned up and got another drink.

Why didn't I tell anyone?

I was underage in a nightclub, drinking. I was dressed in a short skirt. I didn't know who had done it.

If I had told me friends a bloke had "touched me up", they probably would have congratulated me. I could imagine the guy laughing about it with his friends, maybe over a post-club kebab. It made me sick to think that they might have been egging him on, encouraging him, not stepping in to help me. Maybe they were oblivious. If I had told my parents – I couldn't tell my parents, what the hell would they have thought? I certainly couldn't have told my Navy boyfriend!

So, it stayed my dirty secret.

I know now I wasn't to blame. You were not to blame.

But I think it shaped how you related to men over years to come. Latching on to anyone who 'made you' feel special or beautiful or desirable. They knew which buttons to press. Do you remember The Scot (friend of husband #1)? "I can't believe my damn bad luck that I didn't meet you first. I think I'm in love with you. I want you." Cue "fuck buddy" status for the next two years but wouldn't take it any further.

You always thought sex would equal happy relationship, and when it didn't, you found sex elsewhere. The one who wanted to whisk you away to America (until you were found out and you never heard from him again). The one who said, "There's nothing you could ever do to stop me loving you". Gone when things could have developed into a real relationship. Always an excuse. Always a reason to keep you at arm's length. But hey, a good fuck, apparently. Or, willing to have sex with no expectations afterwards, being at their beck and call. Yep, these men "made you" so happy… Where were your needs in this? What about making you happy?

Do you know when you eventually find happiness? When you stop expecting others to make you happy. To coin a phrase, happiness is an inside job. You stop trying to anticipate and predict expectations of the men in your life, as well as others. You stop trying to meet standards that do not exist. You stop trying to be what you think other people want you to be. You stop pinning the success of a relationship on the sex. You stop.

You begin listening to that inner voice and somehow stop measuring yourself against imaginary, shifting goal posts.

So, my thirty-year-old self. Stop. Stop beating yourself up for not being good enough, beautiful enough, sexy enough. Your worth is not measured by the male gaze. Happiness in relationships does not begin and end in the bed.

You are enough.

You are loved.

Take time to listen to what you need and what you want. Happiness will follow, I promise.

X x

"You alone are enough. You have nothing to prove to anybody."

(Maya Angelou)

The Wisdom Within

Dear Anna,

Well, it's a beautiful summer day – endless blue skies, a light breeze. I am sat in my newfound oasis, enjoying a coffee on a day away from work. I am content.

I want to tell you about the mental shift that you experience, which leads to a feeling of peace. I want you to reach it sooner than I did, as so much time was wasted through emotional exhaustion. I have not found this place on my own, it has involved connection with many amazing women, whether that be in real-life friendships, connection on social media, through podcasts or through reading their books. Discovering their journeys, struggles like yours but not the same, how they overcame obstacles and negotiated their demons.

One key thing I've learned is that the voice in your head, telling you that you can't, that you're not good enough, skilled enough; that you're not capable; that if you do or don't do the thing, you'll be letting people down - that voice that draws up imaginary and ever-shifting expectations and goal posts that you constantly measure yourself against – it wants nothing more than to keep you safe. It likes the Comfort Zone, where nothing bad will happen, there is no danger of you embarrassing yourself or failing. Safe from potential criticism when you mess up. Safe from upsetting others and stepping on their toes.

The thing is, I have found that when that inner voice is screaming "NOOOOOOOOO!!" and I do the thing anyway, that is when the magic happens. Whether it was applying for the job or stepping on the stage, to stripping all my clothes off with a group of women I had just met on a hill at sunset (yep, that happens!).

Something incredible happens. A sense of… freedom isn't a big enough word. Liberation, from my own bullshit. And joy! A feeling of weightlessness in my soul.

At thirty, there are so many reasons to listen to that voice – it drives home the guilt about abandoning your motherly duties. Please look for little moments of joy, they are so precious. If the voice is shouting, or reeling off reasons why you can't or shouldn't do the thing, ask it why? What is the worst that can happen?

This is how I started to trust my inner wise woman, my older self. Call it intuition, gut feeling, inner knowing. Call it what you want. She always knows because she has been there. I suppose I am offering myself as your older, wiser self. I admit that I don't always feel particularly wise, but I have learned so much that I want to share my experience with you.

She is the one I can channel and link in with if I am unsure. She is the one who sits back and allows the inner critic, your inner health & safety executive, time to shout and say, "this is why not". Then she quietly takes your hand, looks you in the eye and says "my girl, you can. And I'll show you how." I am feeling quite emotional writing about her, as I have so much to be grateful to her for. She is the one who gently encouraged me to stop when I was trying to be everything to everyone. She's the one who says "rest" when I'm tired but feel guilty for napping. She is the one who was with me in the woods during the photoshoot, encouraging me to embrace the beauty of nature around me and let myself shine amongst it. She is the one telling me I am enough when I start comparing.

So, I will tell you the same:

It is ok to stop. It is ok to rest. Allow your beauty to shine in the world. You, my girl, are enough.

X x

"Embrace the glorious mess that you are."

(Elizabeth Gilbert)

Green Pigs and Other Creations

Dear Anna,

Creativity has always been an important part of our life, but for many years we have stifled its growth. I think we felt that our ideas didn't fit, and at a young age we were criticised for not conforming. I always remember you were in primary school, aged six maybe, reading the Roger Red Hat books, and one day we were asked to colour some pictures from the stories. You were given Jennifer Yellow Hat's front door. The illustrations in the book depicted a plain yellow door between two white pillars. You had a box of crayons in front of you, and you used them all! An amazing rainbow door was created, and you were so happy with it. Until the teacher said "It's supposed to be yellow. You've done it wrong." I remember other children giggling – you had been told off because you didn't stick to the rules.

Later, again in primary school, the class was making papier mâché piggy banks. This involved covering a balloon, attaching egg carton pieces for feet and a snout, and a pipe cleaner for a tail. You painted your pig a vibrant green colour, then decorated it with flowers. It was fabulous! Then your teacher said, "Pigs are not green, are they? They're pink." Your classmates sniggered. You hadn't followed the rules again, you'd done it wrong.

An amazing thing happened in the last year of junior school – Mrs Harvey (your favourite teacher, with her wild grey bobbed hair, her colourful clothes – thinking about her now, the epitome of the Wise Woman!) cast you as the lead in the production of Joseph and his Amazing Technicolour Dreamcoat. The popular girls were not impressed, as you would be centre stage, not them. You had the opportunity to sing in front of the school! It was incredible. You felt that joy, that spark. But you also felt the glare of judgement from others.

Secondary school and college didn't involve much creativity. You studied more academic subjects, not music or art, you hated drama because you feared being laughed at or ridiculed. You enjoyed some crafts – cross-stitch and crochet, but you didn't really share these. Oh, you played the flute! I had forgotten that. Until the age of fourteen, I think, when GCSE studies began. You reached grade 5 but for higher grades would have to study theory, so you let it go. When you were younger, you enjoyed making music, and sometimes gave 'performances' for family (although you would play in a separate room so you couldn't see them watching you). I still have the flute… maybe I could pick it up again?

When your eldest son was born, you painted murals for his bedroom – Winnie the Pooh on his door, and Thomas the Tank Engine on his wall. There was no other outlet for self-expression, and I think where you are now is still stuck. Your interests have focused on those of your partner, and of course our children.

Things do start to change – slowly at first, but you will find things you love, that spark a passion. I remember a day where you try belly dancing at the local summer mela and end up in an impromptu performance in front of the crowd – your photo from that day appeared on the posters for the following year's event!

Through your friend, you are introduced to dancing and burlesque. She helps you find the freedom of expression and a way of channelling your inner confidence through an alter ego, both on and off stage. I do not know if you would have discovered this side of yourself eventually, but she gave you a forum through which to explore and grow and I am grateful for that. You perform on stage (you really do!) which is both terrifying and exhilarating.

You find yoga when your youngest is still tiny, and for a while this is your only outlet. After a few years without practicing, you return to it. I have been to several different teachers, all of whom have given me a different perspective and taught different aspects of yoga, and I find it brings a sense of calm.

You discover you can sew and make simple items with your basic machine. I have recently found a love of painting. I sing spontaneously – often at work, much to my colleagues' amusement! I love photography and being photographed (who would have thought!).

Your creativity also shines in the clothes you wear. For years we have tried to fit in, tried different styles for size, experimented. I have finally come to a point where I wear what feels right for me. I certainly don't fit in, but I no longer care. It is shown through your love of tattoos – I only have five small ones (to date…), two more than those you have. Each tells a story that speaks to you – the dolphin on your hip, the first you had done, once you had separated from husband #1. He hated them, said you "couldn't have them". Well, screw you, mate! The dragonfly on your left wrist, designed by your eldest son when he was fourteen. The butterfly on your belly, barely recognisable through the marks of two pregnancies. The dragon on the small of you back. And your latest addition, a bird flying free from a cage, signifying liberty from the bullshit.

What I want you to know is that you have so much talent and creative spark within you, and you do discover your passions. You will find what makes your heart sing, and you won't be afraid to try. You won't be afraid to colour outside the lines. For so long, we have been afraid of the Others. Of the judgement, the ridicule, the sniggering classmates. Those who mock you are those who are still afraid. Afraid that you can, afraid that you will. They wish they had the courage to not fit in, to try it anyway. To be able to be seen as foolish but enjoy the ride. Our youngest is forever saying I'm 'embarrassing'. He's worried of what the Others will think. I am not anymore. I want to dance along the pavement. I want to paddle in the sea, to climb trees, to go on the swings! I want to paint and sing and feel the joy in my heart when things flow.

When you stop trying to fit in, you find out where you belong.

I want you to know that you will feel it too. Be brave, my girl, let the creativity flow and embrace the joy it brings.

X x

The Importance of Being Grateful

My darling girl,

One thing we discover with time is the importance of gratitude. It is something that comes with practice, and although I don't formalise my daily gratitude practice by writing things down, I feel my mindset has shifted this way. Today, for example, I have a day off work, and it is raining. Others have moaned about the weather, and it could easily bring down my mood. Instead, I am grateful for the rain – I sometimes (often) forget to water the garden, so I am grateful that the plants are receiving much needed water and nutrients. I am grateful that I have a dry house where I can be safe. I am grateful that I can use the time to sit and rest rather than rushing around running errands. I have time to write to you.

Through writing these pages, I realise I have spoken a great deal about past events, but not once do I think I have offered my gratitude to you, my younger self. For a long time, I have looked back at some events with regret, disappointment, beating myself up over decisions and actions taken so many years ago. You made the best decisions you could at the time, for both yourself and your child. You did what you felt was right. You kept going when you could have given up. Thank you for always moving forward, protecting yourself whether through physically removing yourself from situations or by moving on mentally and emotionally. You have carried so much hurt and trauma and will continue to do so but there will come a time where you address it all. By writing to you, the healing process continues. Revisiting past pain and reframing it, letting go of things that no longer serve when moving forward. It is not a quick process.

I spent two years with an amazing counsellor who sat with me and helped me unpick our past. She helped me see another way forward. That it is ok to consider my own needs. To celebrate my successes.

You have so much to celebrate! You have two beautiful boys and three wonderful stepchildren, and they blossom and grow into incredible people. You are part of their growth, your unending support and encouragement. You have a husband who loves and supports you (he may not understand you a lot of the time, but that's where communication comes in). You are starting a job in which you flourish and go on to more specialist roles. You become highly skilled and knowledgeable, an amazing nurse to your patients and role model to your colleagues. You are surrounded by people who love you, and who support you endlessly. You find your cheerleaders as you go through the next chapter.

Thank you for all you have achieved, all your dreams and aspirations. I am where I am today because of you.

With so much love,
X x

The Untold Tales of Motherhood

Dear Anna,

I have been prompted to write to you today about motherhood. You have your two boys – five years old and eight months old. They are now nearly twenty and fifteen, for crying out loud!

What prompted me to write was Mum finding lots of old photos of you with your eldest, just a few hours old. You look elated but exhausted. You wanted nothing more than to nest at home for at least a month, just your little family, but as you had two stepchildren eager to see their baby brother, that wasn't going to happen. Four days after returning home from hospital, you had been whisked to the local shopping mall! Anxious, exhausted, but you were out, and you could do it all! For the first few weeks with your baby, you felt scared. You went to the supermarket with Mum as you were afraid that someone was going to tell you that there had been a mistake at the hospital, he wasn't your baby and they would take him away. Was this normal "new mum" emotion and hormones? Or was something else going on?

You loved being able to breastfeed, you felt so connected with him. Yet you didn't fully feel that he was yours. His father's family were rather overbearing, involved in most decisions in your relationship, and you couldn't really argue as his mum was looking after the baby when you returned to work after just four months. As time went by, baby's dad fell into spells of depression, spending days on the sofa, drinking and smoking. Was he truly caring for your baby when you went to work? You reached out to his family for support, but they enabled him, "He's just in one of his dark moods. It's just him, you'll be fine." You also developed depression and anxiety, and so began your on-off relationship with antidepressants. There were happy times, but they became harder to find. The pressure of supporting the household financially was getting harder with increasing debt. When your boy was three, you left. You would have broken otherwise. Then who would have cared for him?

Eighteen months later, you have your second baby. Another boy. Again, you longed for a period of nesting, but it wasn't to be. Three stepchildren wanted to meet their new brother, as well as your older boy. You desperately wanted to feed him on the breast, but it just wouldn't happen. The guilt you were made to feel by the well-meaning Health Visitors was tough – "You must persist, it's best for baby. Keep trying". You were in so much pain, he was unable to latch on (we now know because he had a slight tongue-tie). The guilt you heaped on yourself when you started him on formula; the fear that you wouldn't have "that connection". But he thrived, gained weight, a healthy baby! When he was five weeks old, Hubby started working nights (timing, eh?). Every day, after being up for the night feeds, you and the boys would walk the streets – to the local shops or the park, so Hubby could sleep. You were soon back on antidepressants for post-natal depression. You return to work after about six months and you fall into a routine. Eldest to his dad's on alternate weekends, stepchildren with you.

And this is where you are now, in a routine of motherly duties and work.

Being short of money is continued stress. The odd dramas with the stepchildren. Your youngest stepdaughter moves in full-time at eleven or twelve. This wasn't in the plan. She has struggled at home, so of course you welcome her, but things feel tricky for a while. Your eldest boy is nine, I think, and he is upset by the changes. Looking back, it was about this time when his behaviour started to change, particularly at school, and his relationship with your husband began to disintegrate. When he starts secondary school, his behaviour becomes almost unmanageable. He is labelled a "troublesome kid" and is almost left to get on with it at school. We later discover he has dyslexia and ADHD. Shouldn't the school have picked that up? He was expelled from this school in year 9, and we were in the process already of transferring to a different secondary school. Thankfully, they still took him. You spend the following few years trying to pour oil on the troubled water that was the relationship between your son and you husband, all the while trying to build a relationship with your stepdaughter. Each of them wants you to be on their side. You can't choose a side! Fractures in relationships widen.

So. Much. Guilt.

You ask them to talk to each other, but they won't. You reach the end of your wits. You book a family counselling session that neither of them wants to attend, but you tell them if it's not sorted "Someone will have to leave, and it might be me." Where did that come from?

The session was fraught (there was only one, they refused to attend again), and they were both angry with you afterwards. Your boy was sent to his dad's for a few weeks (another fraught meeting, this time with his dad and step-mum). You feel like you've lost him, let him down, abandoned him. To your joy, he returns after three weeks, and things change for the better. Relationships slowly heal. Today, he and your husband are good friends.

I realise that I have barely mentioned the younger boy! He is a different child to his brother. A good student at school, generally well behaved and no rebellious streak has shown itself so far (don't want to speak too soon). He has been the constant, grounding presence in this house. He has had a lot to deal with really, observing relationships and battlegrounds. He is curious about things and very knowing. Maybe he has learned the lessons of his elders…

Your relationship with your stepchildren has never been overly maternal, so to speak. They have a relationship with their mum, so didn't need two. You were always there for them, often to pick up the pieces, to talk through things they couldn't talk through with others.

Being a mum has been a joy and has also seen the depths of despair. You have questioned your ability so many times for so many reasons. You have felt taken for granted, that you only shared in the lows whilst viewing the highs on social media. More recently, I have realised that I was seeing the showreel, not reality, and just because everything I do isn't shared for the world to see, it doesn't make it less significant. There were always advisors along the way, telling you how you should parent, how you should relate to your boys, what you should or shouldn't tolerate. They made you feel that you were doing it wrong, making mistakes, creating problems for the future. Telling me how I should and shouldn't let my children relate to me. I have never been a very authoritarian parent, and I am sure I have made mistakes over the years (who hasn't?), but my relationship with them all remains strong.

Our eldest is a qualified mechanic. Studying and academia were never his thing, but give him an engine and a tool kit? His forte. Our youngest will be sitting his GCSEs next year (Covid permitting), then off to college if he chooses. Our stepchildren are also making their way in the world – marketing in media, a lawyer and a nearly-qualified teacher. And two grandbabies! I am so, so proud of them all. And they offer support in return, for whatever project I undertake - going back to university, for example. Mostly, my boys. From babes in arms to hulking six-foot teenagers, they will forever be part of me. My greatest achievements, and the scars to show for it!

Going forward for you, motherhood isn't easy. I won't pretend that it is. Try not to pay too much heed to the "advisors" along the way. You know your boys; you can do this. Along the way, you rediscover glimpses of the 'you' you will become. Keep them in sight, in your mind's eye. You will survive the heartache and will come through with a heart full of pride and love.

They will fly because you supported them in building their wings.

X x

Hopes & Dreams

My dear girl,

Not only are we in the midst of a pandemic, my love, but we are also experiencing a heatwave here in the UK. Temperatures reaching 37°C in other parts of the country, with a 'cooler' 34°C in our town. Thankfully, I haven't been working through the heat, so siestas are now an official part of the daily routine! We did venture to visit the gorillas this week, at our much-loved wildlife conservation park. Gorillas are a great passion, still, and to spend time observing them, occasionally making eye contact with their deep, knowing eyes, always fills my heart with joy.

One of our early dreams was to spend five weeks in Africa on a Land Rover safari, which included sleeping under canvas, visiting five countries, and included a mountain trek in Uganda to see the gorillas. It was booked, deposit paid, holiday agreed with work. Then you met your eldest's dad, soon after, fell pregnant, and that was that. No safari. The dream, however, remains, and I know that I will get to Rwanda. I will. In lieu of Africa, I had a 'keeper for the day' experience at the wildlife park. Oh, it was amazing! To get so close to them, face to face. I cried! The absolute highlight for me was feeding the 7ft silverback a jug of fruit tea. Can you imagine? You do it! The short time seemed to go on for ever, and the connection was incredible. Looking into my face, making little grunts when he was ready for the next mouthful. His hand on the wires separating us, so tempting to rest my fingers on his (strictly forbidden to touch).

I am struggling to remember the dreams of our much younger self. We always hoped for children, and our career aspiration was to become a good nurse. Two dreams ticked off! I would imagine we had also hoped for a romance, a once-in-a-lifetime to spend our days with. The universe had other ideas there. Did we have grand, outrageous dreams? Or did we keep them buried so no one would mock us? I cannot recall all your dreams at thirty: to drive a 1967 Ford Mustang (convertible, in red with cream interior, lots of chrome). To return to Boston, where you spent your honeymoon, for your tenth wedding anniversary. To decorate your bedroom.

None of these have happened yet.

Shall I tell you my dreams, as they are today? To visit Rwanda and my beautiful gorillas. To live in a house that has a terrace overlooking the sea, so I can hear the waves – I see this so vividly! The terrace is filled with plants, with wisteria around the French doors.

I dream that these letters to you will be shared, that someone will read them and take hope or encouragement from them. To succeed in my studies and share my knowledge. To meet in person some of the incredible women I connect with online. To visit Italy, Denmark, Corfu, the Scilly Isles. To remain healthy into old age. To continue to love my family and friends. To have a flourishing, colourful garden.

Some are small, some are big. When I consider each of them, my heart feels full and I feel myself smiling. Dreams and hopes for the future are important, and we are fulfilling some each day. Waiting for the future to find happiness, though, will lead to discontent in the present. Remember I wrote to you about gratitude? It is so important to find things to be grateful for every day, things that bring you joy, or happiness will allude you. Time will pass and we may not achieve that big dream, but we will have found joy on the journey.

X x

Finding My Way

Dear Anna,

I think I have mentioned (a couple of times!) that we are currently living through a pandemic. Covid 19 has taken 2020 as its year of world domination and, though we are no longer under 'lockdown' rules and the second wave hasn't hit as predicted, things are far from normal. As I write, over 40,000 people have lost their lives to this virus in the UK, and we are facing a financial situation on parallel with the post-war recovery of the mid-twentieth century. The country – the world – was pretty much closed for business for three months. People have lost their jobs, their businesses and their hope, in some cases. Children have been out of school since March, although technology has helped with virtual classrooms.

In my corner of the world, I have been lucky. As a nurse, I carried on working throughout. Aside the virus, there were many logistical challenges to be managed, but as a service we kept going and cared for our patients. New rules to follow in terms of physical distancing and PPE, but essentially, we continued. Hubby also continued to work so, financially we have been safe. The youngest boy managed the virtual schooling well, thankfully, and didn't require micromanaging to get it done! Not seeing family was tough, and although technology allowed screen time together, not being able to physically see each other has been heart breaking. Its nearly six months since I've hugged Mum and Dad, and I hate it! As lockdown eased, we have been able to meet up, but 'no touching allowed'. The eldest boy moved in with his girlfriend at the start of lockdown (clearly the perks of being there outweighed those of remaining at home!) so I had to deal with him flying the nest whilst getting my head around the new world. It was hard, and the timing wasn't the best, but they leave, don't they. He knows that this will always be his home, where his roots are, and the door will always be open for him to return should he need to.

Personally – and I appreciate I speak from a position of privilege – I have found great peace from this time of tempestuous change. I had no control over what was happening in the big, wide world, but I could control how I responded to it. I realised quite quickly that watching the news continuously was not good for my mental health. I had to switch off from it. I turned to reading, painting, walking (for my allotted hour a day). I nurtured my garden, as much as it is. I had much more time to just be, and in this space, I felt called to write to you. I also felt called to sit in stillness – the quiet in the garden without the continual thrum of traffic noise. The birdsong. The breeze. I engaged in online classes which prompted reflection, intention and gratitude.

The busyness of 'pre-Covid' had stopped abruptly and could no longer be glorified. I had tried for some time to slow down, but there have often been distractions. Once lockdown arrived, the distractions were gone. So, even though working life continued, life as a whole was calmer. I no longer had to worry about letting people down or how to prioritise. Now restrictions have started to ease, the joy of simple things previously taken for granted is intensified. Having a coffee or a meal with a friend. Playing with my grandbabies. Walking in the woods with family. I haven't felt the pull of the shopping mall or the pub. I haven't missed 'things'. I have missed the real-life connection with those important to me. And if hand sanitiser and face masks mean that I can spend time with those I love, then so be it.

The stillness and peace I have experienced may not have been shared by others. I know others have found the whole experience extremely difficult – high anxiety, isolation, and as I said, I know I am lucky. I hope others will read this, and I wonder what their experience has been like. Have they had an opportunity to reflect on their own pandemic experience? I have learned that being busy is not the aim of living. Being present gives you – gives me – the most out of life, noticing the small things and being grateful to... whoever! God, Mother Earth, the universe, yourself. I have learned that in the stillness, you hear your heart's calling.

Have you heard yours?

With much love, Anna x x

Meeting for the first time

My darling girl,

This week, I had a magical encounter – with myself. I was viewing the images from a photoshoot I had done in a local river. This, in itself, was a wonderful, liberating experience (if a little chilly!), with two other beautiful women and the miracle worker that is Aurora, the photographer. The images thankfully didn't feature blue lips and goosebumps or chattering teeth! What they captured was a woman I did not immediately recognise.

A woman on a bridge in a flowing blue dress, looking radiant and strong. A woman splashing the water looking vibrant and playful. A woman laying the water looking sultry and fierce. And a woman smiling so widely and laughing so openly, she looked both in control and completely unbound. Present in the moment and free to express her true self.

That woman was me.

Whilst looking at the images, it was like meeting myself for the first time. It was clearly me in the photographs, but an unrestrained, more authentic me.

And I love her!

She looks like the woman I have been aspiring to be. Unaffected by rules and expectations. Untamed from years of conditioning to be how she should be.

I remember a photoshoot you had; you were about thirty-two. It was in a studio, you had your hair and makeup done, and you were 'posed' in a series of rooms. You wanted to be sexy, glamorous, desirable. The photos weren't for you, they were for the Others. You were constrained by the studio's portfolio and couldn't express your true self. I don't know what you would have done if you had been given that freedom of expression. You didn't know your true self or how to show her to the world. You certainly wouldn't have stood near-naked in a river!

I wonder what you think about my exploits, being photographed in such a way, purely for myself. The Others these days don't fully understand it; there are a few in the tribe who embrace these opportunities. I am so thankful for the tribe, a group of women I have come to know and connect with, largely online. Without them, I wonder whether I would have come back to myself as I have.

I want you to know that you are that woman. You have a spirit inside you willing you to become untamed, unrestrained, unbound from convention and the rules of the Others. Difficult to picture, right? I couldn't picture it just a year ago, let alone at thirty; I had no idea that she existed.

She does, my love.

She exists. She is willing you forward, desperate for you to see who you really are.

You are fierce, radiant, strong, vibrant and playful.

Anna, meet Anna. As I have finally done.

She is magnificent.

With much love,
X x

My darling Anna,

I have written over several pages about many aspects of, and experiences from, our life which have given me pause to reflect. Throughout my letters, I feel I have not been alone in my writing. I feel that some of these words belong to my older wiser self; my inner mentor who I wrote about. Reading the words back, I hear two voices. My voice, at forty-four, describing events that have happened over our life, and her voice, with a more reflective and understanding tone, offering her words as a means of hope and encouragement to you. Life is hard for you now, and to be honest, it will not get easier for a while to come. It is certainly not always easy for me! What changes is the way in which you perceive the events around you; the way you listen to and filter the voices of others; the way you listen to yourself. And that is the important bit. Listening to yourself, your heart, and what it needs and desires. And not giving a shit about what others think about how you live your life! Their opinion is a reflection of themselves and not about you at all. So, when you feel the urge to buy that unusual outfit, but worry about what others will think of it, buy it. You want to sing in the office? Sing! You want to paddle in January? Do it! Read the obscure books, listen to the strange music, paint your pigs green, dance to the beat of your own damn drum! You will find your tribe.

   Look after yourself, my darling, and everything else will follow.

With so much love and gratitude to you,
Anna x x

"You do not have to relive old stories. Be brave, darling. Write something new."

(S. C. Lourie)

So, dear reader,

You have come to the end of my letters. I have found the process of reflection a positive one. Writing has given me an opportunity to revisit experiences with older, wiser eyes, and the understanding I now have of why I made some decisions. I needed to tell myself that they were the right choices at the time, as I know thirty-year-old me was beating herself up over many of them.

My hope is that some of my experiences will resonate with you and give you an understanding perhaps of your own stories; that these letters make you feel encouraged and hopeful going forward. Maybe you feel inspired to write your own letters? To speak to a younger or older version of yourself, as a means of unravelling experiences or thoughts, of finding the courage to move forward? Maybe you will set aside some time to reflect on where you are today, and notice the small things for which you are most grateful?

My hope is that you start to find joy in your everyday life, and dream of a future which makes your heart sing.

Thank you again for choosing my book. I hope you take some of it with you as you go forward into your wonderful life.

With much love to you,

Anna x x

Aurora Way
@auroraphotographic
@libertyphotographyuk

Lightning Source UK Ltd.
Milton Keynes UK
UKHW010632120321
380227UK00001B/256